To Lenny & Kathy.

Fair Winds and
Smooth Sailing.
at The Mooring.
and beyond.

We enjoyed our
meal. 9/16/00 after
boatshow

Capt. Randy Deering
& Pat

(Friends of Jeff & Elaine)
Come See us when
your in St. Pete, FL

WG

The Sailor's Guide to Life

The Sailor's Guide to Life

Twelve Timeless Principles Based on
Lessons from the World of Sailing

Compiled and Edited by Randy Deering

WALNUT GROVE PRESS
Nashville, TN 37211

ISBN 1-58334-001-7

The ideas expressed in this book are not, in all cases, exact quotations, as some have been edited for clarity and brevity. In all cases, the author has attempted to maintain the speaker's original intent. In some cases, material for this book was obtained from secondary sources, primarily print media. While every effort was made to ensure the accuracy of these sources, the accuracy cannot be guaranteed. For additions, deletions, corrections or clarifications in future editions of this text, please write WALNUT GROVE PRESS.

Printed in the United States of America
Cover Design: *Tal Howell Design*
Typesetting & Page Layout: *Sue Gerdes*
Editor for Walnut Grove Press: *Alan Ross*
1 2 3 4 5 6 7 8 9 10 • 99 00 01 02 03 04

For Pat
My wife and first mate for life

Table of Contents

INTRODUCTION

Sailors are a peculiar lot — different from other boaters. The pace of the sailor, unlike power boaters, is slow and easy. Sailors tend to be more self-sufficient, relying on their boat-handling skills to travel from here to there and back again, no matter the direction of the winds. The best sailors develop an acute feel for the elements of nature, being at one with wind and waves.

Whenever we "go down to the sea in ships," we are confronted with countless learning opportunities; this book addresses some of them. The quotations herein celebrate the joys, the adventures, and even the difficulties of sailing. The words of renowned sailors, writers, philosophers, and leaders remind us of the timeless principles that apply to sailing and to life.

Christopher Cross sang, "Sailing takes me away to where I always wanted to be." And if the place you want to be is the water, the ideas in this book apply to you. Whether you skim around on the local lake, cruise along the coast, or set out on a blue-water voyage to distant lands, the lessons are the same: be prepared, do your best, persevere. And above all, enjoy the sail.

LESSON 1: PRACTICE

Sailing Fundamentals

Watching a sailboat glide smoothly across the water is a beautiful sight — but it doesn't teach sailing. Reading books can be helpful, but a full bookshelf does not a sailor make. Talking to knowledgeable navigators can be insightful, but all the insight in the world can never take the place of experience. In short, one learns to sail on the water — in a sailboat.

The best sailors take sufficient time to learn the fundamental aspects of water and craft. From knot-making to weather-predicting, everything comes easier with practice. Eventually, the captain, having mastered the fundamentals, knows the satisfaction of doing his job right and seamanlike.

Learn of the little
nautilus to sail,
Spread the thin oar,
and catch the
driving gale.

Alexander Pope

Practice is the best of all instructors.

Publilius Syrus

All human virtues increase and strengthen
themselves by the practice
and experience of them.

Socrates

Windward performance remains important
but the need is for good all-around
sailing knowledge and qualities.

Hal Roth

All things are difficult before they are easy.

John Norley

Knowing your vessel is everything;
   each one is a law unto herself. Some pretty
fancy maneuvering can be done by a skipper
who has learned his ship's idiosyncrasies.

Donald Hamilton

One day of practice is like one day
   of clean living. It doesn't do you any good.

Abe Lemons

The most instructive experiences are those
            of everyday life.

Friedrich Nietzsche

First, master the fundamentals.

Larry Bird

We learn the ropes of life by untying its knots.

Jean Toomer

What we need is
someone who can show us
how to tie a clove hitch or
set a whisker pole.
Life is an apprenticeship.

Richard Bode

Bringing a boat neatly
alongside, or putting her
accurately into a slip,
is what really separates
the real sailors from
the landlubbers.

Donald Hamilton

Long ocean passages usually don't require an engine; it's the ports and headlands at each end that may demand some expert sailing.

Hal Roth

Like navigation, anchoring is 60% the science of hard facts, 35% practice and judgment, and 5% luck.

Hal Roth

The truth is that to sail, to even contemplate sailing, calls for a fundamental faith in one's self.

Richard Bode

One of the benefits of depending almost exclusively on sails is that you'll have the joy of working into the same anchorages that Columbus, Drake, Cook and Nelson entered under sail alone.

Lin and Larry Pardey

The fundamentals of boat and sail handling
are easier to describe than accomplish. The
very best way to learn and master them is to
go out and practice them.

John Rousmaniere

There is no substitute for hard work.

Thomas Alva Edison

Nothing is particularly hard if you divide it
into small jobs.

Henry Ford

Match your strategy to your skills.

Arnold Palmer

With repetition comes good habits, with good habits comes good seamanship, with good seamanship comes security, and with security comes enjoyment. And after all, isn't that what we're looking for in the first place?

John Rousmaniere

The sea being smooth,
how many shallow
bauble boats dare sail
upon her patient breast.

William Shakespeare

LESSON 2: PRECAUTIONS

Sailor Beware

No competent sailor would put to sea in an unsound boat. Nor would he go out in a boat without a thorough knowledge of its construction and its equipment.

Careful planning is essential for those who wish to avoid collisions with shorelines, docks and other boats. And steering clear of bad weather and coral reefs is paramount for a successful voyage.

Good sailors are well-prepared sailors; good sailors are careful sailors; good sailors are alert and cautious. The ideas on the pages that follow remind us that careful planning is necessary for a successful voyage on — and off — the water. So sailor beware: What you *don't* know might hurt you *and* your boat!

There is no substitute for a rested and wide-awake person on watch.

Hal Roth

A collision at sea can ruin your entire day.

Thucydides

The elation that is felt at speed, running before the wind and sea, may be so great as to overcome the seamanlike caution the ocean demands, but sooner or later the sea will catch up with you.

Hal Roth

No matter what the type of vessel, she will be thrown around; every moment has to be made with care.

Tristan Jones

Shipwrecks will not wait; the sea is a pressing creditor. An hour's delay may be irreparable.

Victor Hugo

Trouble faced at a time and place of your own choosing is far better than a surprise attack at sea during a storm.

Herb Payson

Prevention is, as in other aspects
of seamanship, better than cure.

Robin Knox-Johnson

If you can't repair it, maybe it shouldn't be
on board.

Lin and Larry Pardey

Boats frequently get into trouble not because
a major piece of gear, like the mast or helm,
breaks down, but because a relatively small
damage or a seemingly minor oversight
creates a chain effect that leads, one link
at a time, to catastrophe.

John Rousmaniere

No amount of skill, no
equipment, and no boat
will keep you from disaster
if you don't develop the
most important seagoing
skill of all, a complete fear
of falling overboard.

Lin and Larry Pardey

It is far better to spend one more lumpy, safe night at sea than to stand on in, risking your vessel and everyone aboard, just for the sake of reaching smooth water, or to be able to say you got in a day earlier.

Ross Norgrove

Handling a sailboat in rough weather demands an attitude of supreme caution. The constant refrain "one hand for yourself, one hand for the ship" neatly summarizes the best approach to staying vertical.

John Rousmaniere

Sailing can fall into a deadly routine that can be called boat-fever which usually responds to a mix of laughter, song, variety, and privacy.

John Rousmaniere

Cruising sailboats are asymmetrical and therefore handle poorly at low speeds. You'll never be bored while docking and undocking.

John Rousmaniere

Evaluate advice from strangers carefully.

Hal Roth

Steadfastly refuse
to upset yourself
over something
you can't control.

Jim Walter

LESSON 3: PERSPECTIVE

Know the Sea, Know the Boat, Know Yourself

There is a story of a man who misjudged the weather, goofed up his navigation, got into trouble, lost his nerve, and called the Coast Guard to rescue him. Yet he considered his cruise a huge success. On the other hand, the famed Sir Francis Chichester sailed alone across the Atlantic and back at age 70, saving his boat by a magnificent feat of seamanship and endurance. But Sir Francis considered his venture a failure because he hadn't achieved his goal of sailing 4,000 miles in 20 days.

In sailing, as in life, success is relative: Each of us must define it for ourselves.

We live in a world where success is elusive and danger may lie just over the horizon. Perspective is an invaluable asset. Good sailors know the sea, their boats, and themselves. And the very best sailors know enough to keep things in proper perspective, as the following quotations will attest.

Who can feel poor when the sails are full and the spirit is full?

Herb Payson

There's one thing about bashing to windward. You never forget, for one minute, that you are at sea in a sailing boat.

Tristan Jones

A cruising life is challenging, interesting, full of variety, sometimes exciting, sometimes frightening, but it's rarely easy.

Lin and Larry Pardey

The long way around is often shorter if the detour takes you away from strong head winds and adverse currents.

Hal Roth

Give wind and tide a chance to change.

Richard E. Byrd

The sea knows awareness, she knows patience,
she knows staunchness, she knows foresight,
yet she knows nothing of man's longing
for riches or fame or even of his efforts
to overcome or to thwart her.

Tristan Jones

Certainly every man that goes to sea in a little
boat learns terror and salvation, happy living,
air, danger, exultation, glory and repose at the
end; and they are not words to him but realities
which will afterwards throughout his life give
the mere words a full meaning.

Hilaire Belloc

Sailing alone around the world, I risked losing
a life that had at last become fulfilling; but in
carrying it out I experienced a second life, a life
so separate and complete it appeared to have
little relation to the old one that went before.

Naomi James

Thunder is impressive;
but it is lightning
that does the work.

Mark Twain

Perspective

It is the individual who knows how little he knows about himself who stands a reasonable chance of finding out something about himself before he dies.

S. I. Hayakawa

Yesterday is a cancelled check; tomorrow is a promissory note; today is the only cash you have — so spend it wisely.

Kay Lyons

Sound judgment with discernment is the best of seers.

Euripides

A right judgment draws us a profit from all things we see.

William Shakespeare

One of the best temporary cures for pride and affectation is seasickness.

Henry Wheeler Show

How holy people look when they are seasick.

Samuel Butler

Sailing often consists of extended periods of relative ease punctuated by brief moments of legitimate fear.

John Rousmaniere

Nothing is worth more than this day.

Goethe

Perspective

When a man comes to like a sea life,
he is not fit to live on land.
Dr. Samuel Johnson

Was there ever a sailor free to choose
that didn't settle somewhere near the sea?
Rudyard Kipling

Seasoned seagoers seem to forget that even
a little gale looks like the end of the world to
the beginner on his first offshore cruise.
Donald Hamilton

Sailing does this for me! The world leaps
into my eyes and ears, touches me in private
places, and afterwards I return to the
mainstream of my life renewed.
Herb Payson

Tragedy and comedy are but two aspects
of what is real, and whether we see the tragic
or the humorous is a matter of perspective.

Arnold Beisser

When ancient opinions and rules of life
are taken away, the loss cannot possibly be
estimated. From that moment, we have no
compass to govern us, nor can we know
distinctly to what port to steer.

Edmund Burke

Stay close enough to the pulse of life to feel
its rhythm, to be comforted by its steadiness,
to know that life is vital and one's own minute
living is a torn fragment of the larger cloth.

Marjorie Kinnan Rawlings

Thought is the wind, knowledge the sail, and mankind the vessel.

August Hare

When defeat comes, accept it as a signal
that your plans are not sound, rebuild those
plans, and set sail once more toward
your coveted goal.

Napoleon Hill

They are ill discoverers that think there is
no land, when they can see nothing but sea.

Francis Bacon

Ideals are like stars. You will not succeed in
touching them with your hands, but like the
seafaring man on the ocean desert of waters,
you choose them as your guides, and
following them, you reach your destiny.

Carl Schurz

The human heart is like a ship on a stormy
sea driven about by winds blowing
from all four corners of heaven.

Martin Luther

The man who goes farthest is generally
the one who is willing to do and dare. The
sure-thing boat never gets far from shore.

Dale Carnegie

Twenty years from now, you will be more
disappointed by the things you didn't do than
by the ones you did do. So throw off the
bowlines. Sail away from the safe harbor.
Catch the trade winds in your sails.
Explore. Dream. Discover.

Mark Twain

A sailor without a destination cannot hope
for a favorable wind.

Leon Tec, M.D.

Raise your sail one foot
and you get ten feet
of wind.

Chinese Proverb

If the doors of perception were cleansed, everything would appear as it is, infinite.

William Blake

LESSON 4: PURPOSE
Charting Your Course

An old saying goes: "Sailing is not a matter of life and death. It's much more important than that." Avid sailors agree. In fact, some are so passionate about life on the water that it becomes part of their purpose for living.

Purpose, no matter what form it takes, requires the courage to persevere in spite of difficulties and dangers. Purpose also requires commitment. A sailor commits to a particular course in order to reach his intended destination. The same principle applies on land.

Courage and commitment are powerful moving forces that give purpose to our lives. But without purpose, we tend to drift aimlessly and achieve little. As Seneca observed, "If one doesn't know to which port one is sailing, no wind is favorable." The ideas in this chapter are intended to help you chart your course — and then sail happily into the sunset.

The highest reward for a person's toil
is not what they get for it, but
what they become by it.

John Ruskin

You will become as small as your controlling
desire; as great as your dominant aspiration.

James Allen

To love what you do and feel that it matters:
How could anything be more fun?

Katharine Graham

Whatever you do, do it with purpose;
do it thoroughly, not superficially.

Lord Chesterfield

Did is a word
    of achievement,
Won't is a word of retreat,
Might is a word
    of bereavement,
Can't is a word of defeat.
Ought is a word of duty,
Try is a word
    of each hour,
Will is a work of beauty,
Can is a word of power.

Anonymous

To reach the port of heaven, we must sail sometimes with the wind and sometimes against it, but we must sail, and not drift, nor lie at anchor.

Oliver Wendell Holmes

There are many points on the compass rose.
I had to locate the few that were meant for me
and head for those that summoned me with
a passion, for they were the ones that gave
meaning to my life.

Richard Bode

I had the ambition to not only go farther
than man had gone before, but to go as far
as it was possible to go.

Captain Cook,
On his voyage to the Pacific in Endeavor

Only he who keeps his eye fixed on the
far horizon will find his right road.

Dag Hammarskjöld

The first thing to do in life is to do with
purpose what one proposes to do.

Pablo Casals

There must be more to sailing than the mere setting out to sail from A to B via C. There must be exploration, not only of new areas of the ocean, but also of new parts of yourself.

Tristan Jones

My heart's longings always urge me to undertake a journey, to visit the country of a foreign people far across the sea.

Kevin Crossley Holland

There are maybe thousands of boatmen who never quite manage to go offshore, although they want to very badly. They keep taking just one more boating course, buying just one more chart or piece of equipment, or taking just one more test cruise along the coast.

Donald Hamilton

I wished to live deliberately, to front only
the essential facts of life, and see if I could not
learn what it had to teach, and not, when I
came to die, discover that I had not lived.

Henry David Thoreau

If one advances confidently in the direction
of his dreams and endeavors to live the life
which he has imagined, he will meet with a
success unexpected in common hours.

Henry David Thoreau

For there is a time for every purpose
and for every work.

Ecclesiastes 3:17b

Obstacles are those frightful things you see when you take your eyes off your goals.

Hannah Moore

The superior man is distressed by the
limitations of his ability. He is not distressed
by the fact that men do not recognize
the ability that he has.

Confucius

If you're determined to be governed by fear,
you'll never do anything. If you want to do a
thing badly enough — you'll do it.

Ross Norgrove

You gain strength, courage, and confidence
by every experience in which you really stop
to look fear in the face.

Eleanor Roosevelt

To realize my dream of sailing was a personal
decision of vital importance, for it meant
pulling up deep roots.

Richard J. Vogt

The man who believes he can do something
is probably right, and so is the man who
believes he can't.

Unknown

I like a person who knows his own mind
and sticks to it; who sees at once what is
to be done, and does it.

William Hazlitt

When a man decides to do something,
he must go all the way, but he must take
responsibility. He must know first why he is
doing it and then must proceed with his
actions with no doubts or remorse.

Carlos Castaneda

Cherish your visions;
cherish your ideas;
cherish the music that
stirs in your heart,
for out of them will grow
delightful conditions.

James Allen

I must go down to the sea again, to the lonely sea and the sky. And all I ask is a tall ship and a star to steer her by.

John Masefield

LESSON 5: POSSIBILITIES

Sailing Where You Want to Go

The sea is ever-changing — and *never*-changing: The challenge it presents to the present-day sailor is as powerful as ever. Five centuries after Columbus expanded the limits of the known world, the open ocean still calls — and sailors are still quick to answer.

There are many "points of sail", and a good sailor knows how to harness the wind and trim the sail in order to go anywhere he chooses at the most effective speed and with the least discomfort.

All of us — sailors and non-sailers alike — face endless possibilities of direction. If we are to be successful, we must first learn to navigate; then we must pick a destination and set sail. The ideas that follow will encourage you to consider your own possibilities and chart your course.

Stop the habit of wishful thinking and start the habit of thoughtful wishes.

Mary Martin

Columbus found a world, but had no chart
save one that faith deciphered in the skies.

George Santayana

The sailor responds to the subtle shifting
of the wind, the imperceptible ebbing of the
tide. He changes course. He trims his sheets.
He sails.

Richard Bode

The way of a boat skimming the water,
how free she runs. She is free only when you
have let her fall off again and have recovered
once more her nice adjustment to the forces
she must obey and cannot defy.

Woodrow Wilson

Sailing a boat well harnesses both natural
and man-made elements in a harmony and
balance determined as much by the boat
as by the way you handle her.

John Rousmaniere

It is a very funny thing about life: if you refuse to accept anything but the best, you very often get it.

W. Somerset Maugham

Each of us is great insofar as we perceive
and act on the infinite possibilities which lie
undiscovered and unrecognized about us.
James Harvey Robinson

Great men speak to us only so far as
we have ears and souls to hear them.
Will Durant

Confidence is that feeling by which the mind
embarks on great and honorable courses
with sure hope and trust in itself.
Cicero

The greatest thing about man is his ability
to transcend himself, his ancestry, and his
environment and to become what
he's capable of being.
Tully C. Knoles

Greatness, in the last analysis,
    is largely bravery.

James Harvey Robinson

We grow great by dreams.

Woodrow Wilson

Nothing happens unless first a dream.

Carl Sandburg

The future belongs to those who believe
    in the beauty of their dreams.

Eleanor Roosevelt

We made the decision to implement our
dream, to satisfy a deep longing for the sea.
We have never regretted the decision.

Richard J. Vogt

To accomplish great
things, we must not only
act, but also dream;
not only plan, but
also believe.

Anatole France

Where there is an unknowable,
there is a promise.

Thornton Wilder

The imagination requires a long range.
First of all a man must see, before he can say.

Henry David Thoreau

Genius must have talent as its complement
and implement, just as in like manner
imagination must have fancy.

Samuel Taylor Coleridge

The world steps aside to let any man pass
who knows where he's going.

David Starr Jordan

We have come from somewhere and are going somewhere. The great architect of the universe never built a stairway that leads nowhere.

Robert A. Millikan

Make big plans; aim high in hope and work, remembering that a noble, logical diagram once recorded, will not die.

Daniel H. Burnham

A little theory goes a long way toward developing an understanding of how a sailboat works, but getting in the boat and actually going sailing is more fun.

John Rousmaniere

Small opportunities are often the beginning
of great enterprises.

Demosthenes

Your big opportunity may be right where
you are now.

Napoleon Hill

Intelligence and the spirit of adventure can be
combined to create new energies, and out
of these energies may come exciting and
rewarding new prospects.

Norman Cousins

The right angle to approach a difficult
problem is the "try-angle."

Anonymous

The great thing in this world is not so much where we stand, as in what direction we are moving.

Oliver Wendell Holmes

There are destinations beyond destinations, and so the confirmed sailor goes on tacking forever.

Richard Bode

LESSON 6: PREPARATION

The Float Plan

When a sailor sets out on an extended passage, it's wise to file a float plan with a relative or friend outlining the intended course, destination and estimated time of arrival. Given the length and the course laid out, the savvy skipper will determine what's needed to make the voyage safely, comfortably, and in good time. Adequate provisions and spare parts must be stowed. Water and fuel must be in the tanks. In addition, the proper charts and local cruising guides must be close at hand.

The quotations in this chapter remind us of the need for preparation whether on the water or off. Sailors — and landlubbers — take note.

The readiness is all.

William Shakespeare

For successful sailing, prepare in advance. Do everything possible before you shove off so you can relax afterward.

Carlton Mitchell

A community is like a ship; everyone ought to be prepared to take the helm.

Henrik Ibsen

A sense of independence is one of the great pleasures of a cruising sailor, but it entails certain responsibilities and a measure of foresight. Cruising sailboats must be self-contained; so must cruising skippers be self-reliant.

Carlton Mitchell

When you've done a reasonable amount of homework, accumulated a reasonable amount of equipment, and run a reasonable number of tests and checks, then it's time to go to sea — and keep going.

Donald Hamilton

Preparation

One of the best things about ocean voyaging and cruising is its safety record. Once you sail out of the breakwaters, your own preparations, skill and care will make you safe.

Lin and Larry Pardey

You carry your independence with you in the form of tools, parts, and the knowledge acquired from books, manuals, magazines, other cruising sailors, or best of all, from experience.

Herb Payson

A sound investment for safety and peace of mind is a great stack of up-to-date charts before you set out on a long trip.

Hal Roth

Napoleon certainly did not have ocean sailing in mind when he said that an army marches on its stomach, but the sentiment is equally valid; feeding the crew well is a crucial factor in running a happy boat.

Jimmy Cornell

Learn to use tides and currents
to your advantage.

Lin and Larry Pardey

When you are under sail you must be ready
to leave the instant the winds are fair, day or
night, not always when it's more comfortable.

Lin and Larry Pardey

It is important not to anchor on the first pass
when you are in new waters.

Hal Roth

Riding out a gale isn't the fun part of offshore
cruising, but it's a necessary and inevitable
part, and you should be aware of it before
you leave the dock.

Donald Hamilton

If you continue to sail on the oceans of the
world, sooner or later you will get a blast
of heavy weather. But careful planning can
minimize severe drubbings by
monstrous seas and winds.

Hal Roth

Chance favors the prepared mind.

Louis Pasteur

The plans of the diligent lead to profit
as surely as haste leads to poverty.

Proverbs 21:5

The success of any project tends to match
the effectiveness of its planning.

Richard J. Vogt

Training is everything. The peach was once
a bitter almond; cauliflower is nothing but
cabbage with a college education.

Mark Twain

Failure to prepare is preparing to fail.

John Wooden

There is need of a sprightly and vigilant soul
to discern and lay hold on favorable junctures.

Pierre Charron

If God be your partner, make your plans large.

D. L. Moody

Spectacular achievement is always preceded by spectacular preparation.

Robert H. Schuller

If you cry "forward," you must without fail
make plain in what direction to go.

Anton Chekhov

The essence of a good seaman is one who
can, in accordance with the old definition,
"hand, reef, and steer" — one who knows
what he's doing about the boat, and does it
enthusiastically, while anticipating what
he might need to do next.

Robin Knox-Johnson

This is one of the very few sports whose
techniques never quite match the demands.
Throughout a sailing career, we never stop
finding new skills to master and
new problems to solve.

John Rousmaniere

Genius is the ability to reduce the complicated to the simple.

C. W. Ceran

LESSON 7: PERFORMANCE

Reading the Wind

No matter how proficient a sailor may be at day sailing, his seamanship is rarely put to the test until he goes cruising or participates in a serious race. Then he may find himself maneuvering into a slip in an unfamiliar marina, riding out a blow at anchor in an unprotected bay, sailing at night to a distant landfall, or working at breakneck speed to change sails rounding a mark. Each of these situations calls for skills and quick decision-making beyond that of the ordinary sailor.

Sometimes in the everyday world, we must perform in ways that take us out of our element. On the job, we're given tasks that stretch our abilities and tax our skills. Like careful skippers, we must be alert to the situation, we must learn from others and from our own mistakes, and we must learn to read the winds of change.

In this chapter, we consider performance-enhancing ideas for those who seek to embark upon a voyage to the next level of excellence.

Do or do not.
There is no try.

Yoda,
from Star Wars

I have always admired the ability to bite off more than one can chew — and then chew it.

William DeMille

When you can do the common things of life in an uncommon way, you will command the attention of the world.

George Washington Carver

Whenever you are asked if you can do a job, tell them, "Certainly I can!" — and get busy and find out how to do it.

Theodore Roosevelt

To be at one with the wind
is to be at home
in the world.

Richard Bode

Each honest calling, each walk of life, has its
own elite, its own aristocracy based
on excellence of performance.

James B. Conant

It is by work that man carves his way
to that measure of power which will fit him
for his destiny.

Josiah G. Holland

What the future holds for us depends on
what we hold for the future. Hard-working
todays make high-winning tomorrows.

William E. Holler

Excellence is an art won by training and
habituation. We are what we repeatedly do.
Excellence, then is not an act, but a habit.

Aristotle

There is no romantic daydreaming when beating to windward. Only the skipper's whole mind, body and soul — thrown completely into the fray — will serve to fight the weather and grab the distance.

Tristan Jones

Speed was to me way down on my list of priorities. It certainly came after steadiness, rig safety, hull safety, endurance, and ease of handling. Give me those and I will cross an ocean at one knot quite happily.

Tristan Jones

The trickiest part of a voyage or cruise may turn out to be the short leg between any harbor entrance and dock, both on the way in and on the way out.

Carlton Mitchell

The sail, the play of its pulse so like our own lives: so thin and yet so full of life, so noiseless when it labors hardest, so noisy and impatient when least effective.

Henry David Thoreau

The secret of happiness is not in doing what one likes, but in liking what one does.

James M. Barrie

It is one of the most beautiful compensations
of this life that no man can sincerely try
to help another without helping himself.

Ralph Waldo Emerson

When we work for others, our efforts return
to bless us.

Sidney Powell

Accept the challenges, so that you may feel
the exhilaration of victory.

Gen. George S. Patton

Happiness lies in the joy of achievement
and the thrill of creative effort.

Franklin Roosevelt

I do the very best I know how, and I mean
to keep on doing it to the end.

Abraham Lincoln

As I grow older, I pay less attention to what
men say. I just watch what they do.

Andrew Carnegie

True merit is like a river. The deeper it is,
the less noise it makes.

Lord Halifax

The seasoned sailor stays on the same tack as long as it appears advantageous, and then, at the appropriate moment, pushes the tiller toward the sail and deftly changes direction.

Richard Bode

The goal is not to sail the boat, but rather to help the boat sail herself.

John Rousmaniere

LESSON 8: PERSEVERANCE

Going to Weather

A sailor's axiom states that the wind always comes from the direction you want to go. And every sailor knows that you can't sail directly into the wind. So the alternative is clear: "going to weather" — not the easiest way to sail — tacking through wind and waves. To tack a boat, to sail a zigzag course, is not to forget your destination. Tacking is simply your response to the obstacle of the wind and your determination to make the most of each leg of the journey until you reach landfall.

So it is with life. Often, you face obstacles that stand in the way of success, circumstances beyond your control. During these difficult times, you may, of necessity, veer left or right (port or starboard), but you will also keep your goal in sight. The keys to your eventual success are perseverance, patience, and a willingness to continue working despite temporary diversions.

For timely insights about "going to weather," consider the quotations that follow. And when the seas of life are choppy and the winds blow directly from your destination, just keep on tacking with the certain knowledge that ill winds — and difficult circumstances — are always temporary.

There is some satisfaction
that is mighty sweet
to take,
When you reach a
destination that you
thought you'd never make.

Spirella

Screw your courage to the sticking-place
and we'll not fail.

William Shakespeare

Victories that are easy are cheap. Those only
are worth having which come as the result
of hard work.

Henry Ward Beecher

Without hope there can be no faith; without
faith in the world and in yourself there can be
no true love, no real compassion; and without
compassion there can be no future.

Tristan Jones

Blessed is the man who perseveres under
trial, because when he has stood the test,
he will receive the crown of life that God
has promised to those who love him.

James 1:12

We can do anything if we stick to it
long enough.

Helen Keller

There is no great achievement that is not
the result of patient working and waiting.

Josiah G. Holland

Diligence is the mother of good luck,
and God gives all things to industry.

Ben Franklin

Never give in! Never give in! Never, never,
never, never — in nothing great or small, large
or petty — never give in except to convictions
of honor and good sense.

Winston Churchill

The secret is this:
Strength lies in tenacity.

Louis Pasteur

Deferred joys purchased by sacrifice
are always sweetest.

Bishop Fulton J. Sheen

Press on. Nothing in the world can take
the place of persistence.

Ray Kroc

Nothing can come between me
and the full prospect of my hopes.

William Shakespeare

Genius is one percent inspiration
and ninety-nine percent perspiration.

Thomas Alva Edison

Nothing in the world can take the place of persistence. Persistence and determination alone are omnipotent.

Calvin Coolidge

The credit belongs to the man who strives valiantly; who knows the great enthusiasms and the great devotions, and spends himself in a worthy cause.

Theodore Roosevelt

Bach, with his precise mathematical progressions, is the perfect music for beating to windward and calculating against leeway and current. He shows that with patience and persistence we will arrive eventually, and we can overcome anything.

Tristan Jones

Six days shalt thou labor and do all thou art able, and on the seventh — holystone the decks and scrape the cable.

Richard Henry Dana

A smooth sea never made a skillful mariner. The storms of adversity, like those of the ocean, rouse the faculties, and excite the invention, prudence, skill and fortitude of the voyager.

Author Unknown

The people who get on in this world are the
people who get up and look for the
circumstances they want, and, if they
can't find them, make them.

George Bernard Shaw

Far away there in the sunshine are my highest
aspirations. I may not reach them, but I can
look up and see their beauty, believe in them
and try to follow where they may lead.

Louisa May Alcott

Whatsoever thy hand findeth to do,
do it with all thy might.

Ecclesiastes 9:10

A great pleasure in life
is doing what people
say you cannot do.

Walter Gagehot

He conquers who endures.

Persius

LESSON 9: PROGRESS
Know Where You Are

All sailors chafe at the notion of *not* going someplace: Currents and contrary winds can make for slow, frustrating sailing. But savvy sailors understand that, while the speed of the boat is important, a knowledge of the boat's position is absolutely crucial. Without this information, it's difficult for a sailor to plot his course and determine his progress.

Knowledge of speed, time and distance are essential to navigation. Information about current, wind speed and water depth is helpful, too. Sometimes this information is readily available, sometimes it's not. When a sailor is unsure of his position, he must collect whatever details he can to calculate his location and his progress.

In life, as in navigation, we don't always possess the information we need or want. A master plan simply isn't available. So we sail ahead, looking for signs, gathering facts, learning as we go. In this chapter, we consider various ways of gauging our position and correcting our course.

When any real progress is made, we unlearn and learn anew what we thought we knew before.

Henry David Thoreau

Progress is a tide. If we stand still we will surely be drowned. To stay on the crest, we have to keep moving.

Harold Mayfield

Going with the wind is the most dangerous course of all. It is deceptively easy to be lulled into a false sense of security.

Richard Bode

Anyone can learn to shoot the sun; but to be able, at any time, to put a finger on the chart and say, with confidence, "We are here," one must first be a seaman of long experience, skilled in the art of guessing right, with a power of reasoning out the effect of all the forces of wind and tide and sea.

Weston Martyr

It matters not how small the beginning
may seem to be: what is once well done
is done forever.

Henry David Thoreau

Be very careful, then, how you live — not as
unwise but as wise, making the most
of every opportunity.

Ephesians 5:15–16

Our doubts are traitors, and make us
lose the good we oft might win,
by fearing to attempt.

William Shakespeare

Well done is better than well said.

Ben Franklin

Things may come
to those who wait but
only the things left by
those who hustle.

Abraham Lincoln

To find out what one is fitted to do and
to secure an opportunity to do it
is the key to happiness.

John Dewey

We lack a sure sense of the appropriate
because we haven't taken the time to figure
out where we are.

Richard Bode

The only thing worth having is that which he
gets by his own exertions, and what he gets is
in direct proportion to what he puts into it.

Albert L. Lowell

Though many sailors aim for pinpoint
navigation, they rarely achieve it. Expecting
too much accuracy will lead to frustration,
time-consuming repetitions of bearings and
calculations, and overly optimistic projections
that may cut corners and leave the boat high
and dry on a reef.

John Rousmaniere

Great men are they who see that the spiritual
is stronger than the material force,
that thoughts rule the world.

Ralph Waldo Emerson

At every crossing on the road that leads to
the future, each progressive spirit is opposed
by a thousand appointed to guard
the past.

Maurice Maeterlinck

The price of greatness is responsibility.

Winston Churchill

What's at stake is nothing less than personal
autonomy, our capacity to empower ourselves
so that we may choose the course of our life
rather than have it chosen for us by others.

Richard Bode

Never mistake motion for action.

Ernest Hemingway

In sailing, as in life, momentum is a valued commodity, the secondary source of power that keeps us going long after the original source has disappeared.

Richard Bode

Optimism is the faith that leads to achievement. Nothing can be done without hope and confidence.

Helen Keller

You can't build a reputation on what you're going to do.

Henry Ford

When you blunder, blunder forward.

Thomas Alva Edison

Success is a journey, not a destination.

Ben Sweetland

LESSON 10: PROBLEMS

Weathering the Storm

Every cruising area has its problems. A sailor can suffer sunstroke after grounding in the endless shallows of Florida or suffer a nervous breakdown running his boat on watery Mexican fuel. As one old salt observed, "If boating isn't a bit of a challenge, what's the point?"

Problems are an inevitable and inextricable part of life. In fact, if you're not having some kind of difficulty, you might want to check your pulse.

When you encounter the choppy waters that must, from time to time, swell in every life, remember that today's problems are simply preparation for tomorrow's, and next week's, and next year's.

Sometimes your problems will seem insurmountable. They're not. Sometimes your troubles will seem insoluble. But they aren't. In weathering the storm, you must draw strength from others and keep the faith. Then, like a veteran sailor, you can heave to, batten down the hatches, and ride out the blow. The following quotations tell how...

Being hove to in a long gale is the most boring way of being terrified I know.

Donald Hamilton

The block of granite which is an obstacle
in the pathway of the weak, becomes
a stepping-stone for the strong.

Thomas Carlyle

Trouble creates a capacity to handle it.

Oliver Wendell Holmes

Troubles are only mental; it is the mind that
manufactures them, and the mind can forget
them, banish them, abolish them.

Mark Twain

The cabin of a small yacht is truly a wonderful
thing; not only will it shelter you from the
tempest, but from the other troubles of life;
it is a safe retreat.

L. Francis Herreshoff

There are three marks of a superior man:
being virtuous, he is free from anxiety;
being wise, he is free from perplexity;
being brave, he is free from fear.

Confucius

It is the character of a brave and resolute
man not to be ruffled by adversity
and not to desert his post.

Cicero

All problems become smaller if you don't
dodge them but confront them. Touch a
thistle timidly, and it pricks you; grasp it
boldly, and its spines crumble.

William F. Halsey

The greatest man chooses
right with the most
invincible resolution,
is calmest in storms,
and is most fearless under
menaces and frowns.

Seneca

They cry unto the Lord in their trouble, and he brings them out of their distresses. He makes the storm calm, so that the waves are still.

Psalm 107:28-29

Anyone can hold the helm
when the sea is calm.

Publilius Syrus

In great straits and when hope is small,
the boldest counsels are the safest.

Livy

Failure is the opportunity to begin again
more intelligently.

Henry Ford

Try to learn from your mistakes and from
new situations, be tolerant of your and your
shipmates' minor errors, and do your best
not to make them again.

John Rousmaniere

From the right point of view, every storm
and every drop in it is a rainbow.

Henry David Thoreau

For God has not given us the spirit of fear;
but of power; and of love,
and of a sound mind.

2 Timothy 1:7

A diamond is a chunk of coal that made
good under pressure.

Anonymous

I've suffered a great many catastrophes
in my life. Most of them never happened.

Mark Twain

All difficulties are but
easy when they
are known.

William Shakespeare

Have I not commanded you?
Be strong and courageous; do not be afraid,
nor be dismayed: for the Lord your God
is with you wherever you go.

Joshua 1:9

It is impossible for a man to despair who
remembers that his Helper is omnipotent.

Anonymous

Adversity reveals genius,
prosperity conceals it.

Horace

No problem can stand the assault
of sustained thinking.

Voltaire

Sacrifices are required for the privilege
of floating around free.

Ross Norgrove

A boat's crew is human, hence prone
to make mistakes.

John Rousmaniere

The only good luck many great men ever had
was being born with the ability and
determination to overcome bad luck.

Channing Pollock

All these woes shall serve
for sweet discourses in our times to come.

William Shakespeare

I lift up my eyes to the hills…where does my help come from? My help comes from the Lord…The Lord will keep you from all harm — he will watch over your life.

Psalm 121:1, 2, 7

Courage is grace under pressure.

Ernest Hemingway

The greater the difficulty, the more glory in surmounting it.

Epicurus

There is nothing the body suffers that the soul may not profit by.

George Meredith

LESSON 11: PATIENCE

Be Calmed

There is a zone in both the Atlantic and Pacific Oceans where weather patterns converge producing a flat calm called the "doldrums." When in those zones, a sailor may drift for days until the current takes his boat where there is wind. When the wind does pick up again, as a sailor changes course, there is a frightening moment when he passes through the eye of the wind that is becalmed.

There are times when we all feel becalmed in our lives. We seem to be going nowhere — and each day seems an eternity. It may appear that we are stuck like a "painted ship upon a painted ocean," unable to move toward our desired goals.

In time, the currents of life will lead us to a place where we can move forward again — in better and more energizing ways. Meanwhile, the lessons to be learned in the doldrums — lessons about patience and about ourselves — are well worth the wait.

All human wisdom is summed up in two words: wait and hope.

Alexander Dumas

Adapt the pace of nature;
      her secret is patience.

Ralph Waldo Emerson

Genius is nothing but a great aptitude
      for patience.

Ben Franklin

Teach us O lord, the discipline of patience,
      for we find that to wait is often harder
            than to work.

Peter Marshall

Our real blessings often appear to us in the
shape of pains, losses, and disappointments;
    let us have patience, and we shall soon see
        them in the proper figures.

Joseph Addison

Genius may conceive, but patient labor
must consummate.

Horace Mann

Patience and diligence, like faith,
move mountains.

William Penn

No great thing is created suddenly.

Epictetus

Nature's instructions are always slow,
those of men are generally premature.

Rousseau

A man's wisdom gives him patience.

Proverbs 19:11

All great achievements require time.

David Joseph Schwartz

If you cannot arrive in daylight, then stand off well clear, all night, and wait until dawn. After all, that's one of the things God made boats for — to wait in.

Tristan Jones

Have patience with all things, but first of all
with yourself.

St. Francis of Sales

To do nothing is sometimes a good remedy.

Hippocrates

Let us not become weary in doing good,
for at the proper time we will reap a harvest
if we do not give up.

Galatians 6:9

Keep the time, observe the hours of the
universe. What are three score years and ten
hurriedly and coarsely lived compared to
moments of divine leisure in which your life is
coincident with the life of the universe?

Henry David Thoreau

Nature cannot be tricked or cheated.
She will give up to you the object of your
struggles only after you have paid her price.

Napoleon Hill

Know this, that the trying of your faith
works patience. But let patience have her
perfect work, that you may be perfect
and complete, wanting nothing.

James 1:3,4

Patience permits us to cling to our faith in the
Lord when we are tossed about by suffering
as if by surf. When the undertow grasps us
we realize that we are actually being helped
even as we cry for help.

Neal A. Maxwell

I sit high on the windward deck and tell myself
to watch the sail, watch the wind,
and beware the jib.

Richard Bode

Although routine might sound the wrong
term to describe life at sea, on any well-run
ship, the daily activities of necessity have
an element of routine about them.

Jimmy Cornell

All human power is a compound of time and patience.

Honoré de Balzac

Be patient, for the world
is broad and wide.

William Shakespeare

It is not necessary for all men to be great
in action. The greatest and sublimest power
is often simple patience.

Horace Bushnell

Our patience will achieve more
than our force.

Edmund Burke

The end of the matter is better than its
beginning, and patience is better than pride.

Ecclesiastes 7:8

Patience is the companion of wisdom.

St. Augustine

LESSON 12: PEACE

Safe Harbor

After a long, hard, and sometimes exhilarating "beat" to windward, it is soothing to "fall off" (turn away from) the wind and be pushed gently along. Even more satisfying and peaceful is to drop anchor in a quiet bay or inlet after a long passage.

We work diligently in our lives at producing, achieving, providing — pushing hard to "make it" in a world that places a high value on productivity. What a shame when we live mindlessly, running against the clock, against ourselves, and even against death, missing the essence of living.

All of us crave a feeling of peace, but sometimes that feeling is hard to find. In this concluding chapter, wise men and women describe the safe, peaceful harbors of life. Enjoy.

The sea is a great consoler. She may beguile us, she may challenge us, she may destroy us, but she never refuses us.

Tristan Jones

If it is possible, as much as it is in you,
live at peace with all men.

Romans 12:18

I do not want the peace which passeth
understanding, I want the understanding
which bringeth peace.

Helen Keller

Seek peace, and pursue it.

Proverbs 34:14

But what is happiness except the simple
harmony between a man and the life he leads?

Albert Camus

Behind every man's busyness there should be a level of undisturbed serenity and industry, as within the reef encircling a coral isle there is always an expanse of still water.

Henry David Thoreau

The secret of contentment is the realization that life is a gift not a right.

Anonymous

Guilt is concerned with the past.
Worry is concerned about the future.
Contentment enjoys the present.

Anonymous

Happiness ain't a thing in itself — it's only a contrast with something that ain't pleasant.

Mark Twain

But godliness with contentment is great gain.

1 Timothy 6:6,7

Happiness is not a matter of events, it depends on the tides of the mind.

Alice Meynell

Everything significant is small and slow.

Richard Bode

I have learned how to be content
in whatever state I am.

Philippians 4:11

Sometimes the Lord calms the storm;
sometimes He lets the storm rage
and calms His child.

Anonymous

When peace like a river attendeth my way,
When sorrows like sea billows role,
Whatever my lot, he hath taught me to say,
It is well, it is well with my soul.

Horatio O. Spafford

Peace

With ghosting sails we can glide along over
water that scarcely shows a ripple and the
feeling is one of calmness and tranquillity.

Hal Roth

The dream I had long held was to voyage
afar in a sailing boat; to see people and places
in a manner possible by this means; to move
in humble harmony with the sea and the wind
and to count these formidable elements as
my friends; to encounter new experiences,
discover new values, and to enrich my life.
I have found these things.

Richard J. Vogt

It is more important to live the life one
wishes to live, and to go down with it
if necessary, quite contentedly, than live
more profitably but less happily.

Marjorie Kinnan Rawlings

Life and economics, as well as health,
run in cycles, so we must be able to handle
the bitter with the sweet.

J. E. Adams

The grass is greenest right where you are.

Wally "Famous" Amos

A single grateful thought raised to Heaven
is the most perfect prayer.

Gotthold Ephraim Lessing

If there is to be any peace it will come
through being, not having.

Henry Miller

Nothing can bring you peace but yourself.

Ralph Waldo Emerson

A contented mind is the greatest blessing
a man can enjoy in this life.

Joseph Addison

Be good, keep your feet dry, your eyes open,
and your heart at peace.

Thomas Merton

A heart at peace gives life to a body.

King Solomon

Courage is the price that life extracts
for granting peace.

Amelia Earhart

Have courage for the great sorrows of life
and patience for the small ones; and when
you have laboriously accomplished your
daily task, go to sleep in peace.
God is awake.

Victor Hugo

When we have done our best,
we should wait the result in peace.

J. Lubbock

A sailor's joys are
as simple as a child's.

Bernard Moitessier

Sources

Sources

Sources

About the Author

Randy Deering is a licensed Captain and sailing instructor living in St. Petersburg, Florida. He also leads seminars and workshops on subjects related to management, supervision, and leadership development. *The Sailor's Guide to Life* is Deering's first book for Walnut Grove Press.

About Wisdom Books

Wisdom Books chronicle memorable quotations in an easy-to-read style. This series provides inspiring, thoughtful and humorous messages from entertainers, athletes, scientists, politicians, clerics, writers and renegades. Each title focuses on a particular region or area of special interest.

If you enjoyed this book, you will also enjoy *The Fisherman's Guide to Life* by Dr. Criswell Freeman. For more information about that book and other titles by Walnut Grove Press, please call 1-800-256-8584.